Bird of Sorrow

Acknowledgements

Grateful acknowledgement is made to the editors of the publications in which some of these poems first appeared: *Orbis*, *Peleton*, *Mill*, *Ink Sweat &Tears*, *Mslexia*, *Envoi*, *The Indian Quarterly*, *Southbank*, *Iota*, *PN Review*.

'Bird of Sorrow II' (Medea's Song) was commended in the PN Review Prize 2017.

My thanks go to Laura Scott and Tista Austin for reading drafts of certain poems and offering encouragement and advice; to Jane Weir for reading this manuscript with sensitivity and kindess; to Mimi Khalvati, a remarkable poet whom I am have been lucky to count as my teacher; to Dayanita Singh whose art and conversation provide invaluable nourishment; and to Emi Takahashi Tull and Michael Saunders whose guidance helps me in too many ways to innumerate. Finally, thanks to Michael Rosas Cobian for his love, support and the generosity with which he allows me to draw ideas from his own beautiful practice.

By the same author

Poetry

Furies (2016)

Essays and Conversations

Interview with Adrienne Rich published in *Arts of the Possible* by Adrienne Rich (WW Norton, 2001)

Dawn's First Cold Breath published in *Vicken Parsons: On Reflection* (Ivory Press, 2017)

Bird of Sorrow

Rachel Spence

Templar Poetry

Published in 2018 by Templar Poetry

Fenelon House
Kingsbridge Terrace
58 Dale Road, Matlock, Derbyshire
DE4 3NB

www.templarpoetry.co.uk

ISBN 978-1-911132-36-3
A CIP catalogue record of this book is available from the British Library

Typeset by Pliny

Cover Design and Artwork by Templar Design

Printed in England

For

My parents, Jack and Sue

' "The waters have produced" [Gen 1: 20] these signs, but only through your word.'
Confessions, Saint Augustine

"We have ancestors in common with butterflies and larches."
Seven Brief Lessons in Physics, Carlo Rovelli

Contents

BIRD OF SORROW I

The bird of sorrow is celibate
        as unshed ink. Her body hides
behind itself. She is waiting
        for dusk to depart in a flurry
of dishevelled blue. Nobody
        comes here now. Except
the old man with his broom.
        He whispers of white light
bunched around a woman's
        navel. The dust listens. Makes
notes. So many missing sisters!
        The bird unfolds her wings
as a saint opens his hand.
        Her alibi is the sea but do not
mistake her for a shell.
        She has spent long nights
with Lazarus. Who knew the clotted,
        white gleam of morning would burn
so harshly? Now she is blind,
        her flight inward, unblinking.

BIRD OF SORROW II

i

She remembers islands. Grids that refuse
language

        Some idea of happiness

ii

Her task is to unstitch time, lay it on the beach
in bolts of raw, unpicked cotton

        the women singing
the hobbled syntax of exile

        Her gaze rakes
the horizon   she is seeking the books
    packed in leaky crates
        vulnerable as turtles
making a run for the sea

iii

She remembers doves. Kings leaping
into the childless blue. A time when
the circle was the perfect expression
of justice

She has bitten her nest
out of the rock. She's deep
in border country, untenanted
ground. A land where long-eyed women

sew lengthwise and crossways

                              Do not
trespass. Do not step on the cracks

                    Soon, she will reach
the blue peninsula

                Her chicks will levitate

GIRL, RISING

The girl rises. Her lodestone is

       is the moon. In a city where

thresholds are porous, she lacks

       even a doorframe. Only light

and shade stay separate here.

       Between the piebald thatching

of the sea and darkness

       cooling in the dunes

lie traps for gravity.

       Later, in another city, you'll

find the missing doorway

       empty, numinous, whispering

that we are only files

       of light archived billennia ago.

Who watches us? Where? When?

FUGITIVE

Daybreak, the cathedral of Torcello,
light skinning the darkness from the windows,
glass lending your blue the fugitive touch of water.

Imagine a cave at midnight in the core of the mountain,
that's how deep you've kernelled your migrant knowledge,
nomad wisdom.

I think you were here before time,
before the rivers mingled with the sea.
They say your seed was planted in Jerusalem,

an era when you could reach back into history
and touch its fulcrum as it makes that slow,
perplexing pivot from truth to legend.

(Had you known you'd never
have worn that old blue gown,
your sister's hand-me-down.)

Luke said it didn't matter,
just the two of you alone in that upstairs room
in the old city, in a time before bells.

Nothing of that survives,
his goal was never likeness,
it was witness.

He told you to raise one hand and point,
he never said he'd add the baby later,
just one more someone who couldn't say His name.

A caesura that lasts centuries, dismantles gods.
Until what is left is you and your brittle, golden doll:
She who points the way.

And now you're here, on the threshold
of a city also burdened by an excess of declensions,
your truth as fleeting as the sheen of your sister's gown.

MAPPINGS (TORCELLO SONG)

i

A face in the street is mistaken for a friend,
and the day is sutured with its repetition.
Brow and cheekbone and twist of smile
seeded in a travesty of recognition.

ii

Is this why today I need the roots of words?

Trace the source of grace back to the Latin.

Gratia. A pleasing quality.

To find your voice in a fossil buried close to Our Lady.

Mosaic from *mouseios*

belonging to the Muses

Her robe the colour of deep sea over rocks.

Outside, the air is damp with mosquito kisses.
The last comma of sunset licking the crab nets.

Love stripped to plainsong.
Language to hieroglyph.
Icon to portrait.

Tomorrow free from intimacy in the faces of strangers.

FIRST NIGHT

Piazzale Roma, Venice.
The Grand Canal furred by a ruff of mist.
Only in January, these chiffonned nights.
Evening boiled down to jaundiced vapours
and smears of sepia light – on lamp-posts,
behind windows, hand-held on boat prows
by men who read the weather like a lexicon
of wind speed and direction, tide, current,
visible distance. Fog just one more dialect
though nowhere does pea soup like Venice.
As if the witches were waiting on the heath,
palaces riding the exhale of a diseased lung,
faultlines cracking in our weary hearts.
No Hitchcock to say cut.

Outside The Bakery

Saturday, 10am, the Street of the Cats.
Morning hammered thin by rain, paving stones
licked by bronze. Outside the bakery,
four ladies boneless as the loaves in their trollies,
tossing a recipe for meatballs through the rusty air.
A man passes, his cheeks pouched with middle-age.
"Angelo!" calls a lady. "I saw your mamma yesterday.
Why do you never visit her?" Chastened, he bows
his head, taking his scolding from a woman
for whom St Mark's Square is as far as Paris, unaware
that fifty years ago his mother was the local beauty,
a Titian blonde in swing skirt and stilettos,
that the bread buyers hissed "*putana*"as she passed.

LIZARD

That summer was slimy-hot; the air a damp broth
even under a ceiling made for acrobats.

One afternoon, my skin greased from the fan's brew,
I saw a lizard flash along the wainscot,

a minnow of dark light, a film of displaced dust,
thin as the skin between laughter and tears.

Weeks later, I woke at dawn to scuffling:
curious, foreign, Polanski-sinister.

I lay there waiting for the wall to crack,
curtains to buckle in an absent wind,

while the lizard said farewell and the first chord
of autumn blew in from the sea.

CORTE SCONTA

Our hands clasped across the table;
a prayer of fingers, text of flesh,

wrestling need out of the mute oak.
It could be Paris, Dakar, ancient Rome.

We have built a pyramid of blame,
stacking fault with the precision of children.

The waiters drop their charm offensive;
the rose seller gives us a wide berth.

Certain of victory, Language slinks off.
Our world cropped to the theatre of cutlery.

And you take my hand. Silence ruptures.
A couple close to us starts to quarrel.

SHIP OF FOOLS

Bound together at the helm
of that black, broken deck
of water, blind to the bridal
moon, we followed the stars.
Absent, treacherous messengers,
pregnant with dead light.

Hard City

Night has left me raw. Heart-stalked.
Betrayals aggravated by their minor nature.

I wake to silence damp with the canal's secrets.
A gull boomerangs across the sky's blue wing.

Fumbling to catch thoughts like dropped stitches,
I stumble out into a morning made snappish

by its own beauty. The neighbourhood hugging
her pigments like spells: ochre; madder; ultramarine.

In the water, palaces hang like prints in a darkroom;
everybody stunned by fishbowl stillness.

You should know this is a hard city.
Somewhere a shift in the wind

can set even the dogs sulking. The pull of the tide
make you plot against your familiar.

You'll turn blind in your dreams,
wake speaking in tongues, look up from the stove

to find your child swapped for another;
a renunciation you can't remember making.

AFTER YOU'D GONE

i

The nights I stayed awake, listening to the snores of the old man
on the far side of the canal, lovers quarrelling on the bridge
below my window, their voices trapped, dilated,
by the echo chamber of the water's throat.

                  I'd leave the window wide, uncurtained.
Nothing but threshold. Confessional hour for exiles and angels.
Those who know that you can burrow into smell or light.
Your unwashed skin. The sullen blink of moss.

                  Mystical protocols for liminal people.

Lick. Look. Lap.

ii

In the blood-sugar dip of dawn, rat's bony, spectral plop.
Ribcage of barge moaning as the rope pulls tight
against the swell.

                  A time when dreams showed me to myself
as blind, a boy, staggering over the devil's bridge, not knowing
that it marked the blue way out of here.

                  I am learning that water has its own pulse,
fluid of the instinct-driven body, blood and the flowing of blood.
I am learning to live in the redshift hour.

                      The place on the map where the road
runs out. The Japanese engravers practising over and over
the stuttering line where the painter's brush falters for lack of ink.
These replicas of absence requiring years to master.

VENICE, AUGUST

i

So damp my bedroom could be lined
with moss

    even the bells sound waterlogged

in the garden, every animal has its own hour

the blackbird comes at dawn, rising
                     and falling
                     as if on strings

at noon, the cat with topaz eyes slips through
the lattice fence

only the lizards move freely
and they are less than light

ii

Every morning, the woman upstairs
sweeps her balcony as I sit below
trying to write. She has grey hair,
a housedress in blue and white,
but I can't see her face through
the leaves

If she passed me in the street, I would fail
to say *buon giorno*

                      city of tripwires, dry

with longing

          the bell ringers submerged, holding

their breath

PALERMO SUITE

RIGHT TO CHOOSE I

Madonna of triangles: perfect V
of flesh above your breastbone,
pyramid of cloak carving diagonals
out of the vowel of black. In an era
when geometry seemed God's own arithmetic,
perspective set you free as a night swimmer.
Then Antonello turned you inwards;
he dusted you with lamp-black,
made you edgeless in an edgeless world.
You are L'Annunziata
but your raised hand announces
that your womb will stay empty
as the darkness streaming behind you,
centuries of women holding their starless breath.

ANTONELLO'S SONG I

I was born in harbour light —
porous, transient.
No wonder Venice spoke to me.

But I had changed by then.
In Tuscany, I met Piero,
his Mary's face blank as her pregnant belly,
an inland light, made for the plainsong
of the Tuscan hills, depth not ruled
but sung, form made
and unmade, until the eye learns to let go
find unity
            in anklebone and column,
brow and archivolt.

I was too good a pupil.
Piero would have made an offering
to the tangible:
shine bouncing off a pearl,
a little sigh of pattern.

My model's face said otherwise.

I found her selling eggs,
cheek mapping shell,
all around us the hysteria of market
and this girl,
            still as the afternote of a bell.

In Italy, we've drawn God into being.
Vittoria comes from somewhere else,
a place where He cannot be shown,
as if her bones had cancelled themselves out.

Antonello's Song II (On a Line by Dionne Brand)

I painted her in Venice,
        somewhere an absent light
warns of the rain to come
        and you can sleep with
a woman you'll never
        meet again yet step into
the vinegar plume
        of her scent hanging
in an alley hours after
        she has passed. Love
dried out by the monstrous
        wisdom of a city built
on water where pigments
        are sold in apothecaries'
shops and painting
        can heal you even as
the sky above the *calle*
        stretches to the Dolomites,
that mineral blue
        soaked out of lapis lazuli
from Persian caves,
        one mountain lending its language
to another, painful translations
        that leave you thirsty

VITTORIA'S SONG

Madonna, he was arrogant!
Here, where there's a painter
for every fisherman,
he thought I'd gone unnoticed.
(Those Bellini boys bought eggs
enough to feed the army *torta*
for a month.)
I sent them all away –
my face an architecture of the no,
he says…
but how could I resist that swallowing darkness
in a city where light has too many tenses
          to be desired
illegible   but not illiterate

The cloak was mine, curfew-blue and soft
as my best hen when I lift her from the lay.
I saw the lapis though –
just looking at it made me want
          to pray.
Nothing of that colour
               ever came into our house.
Falling in love
           like stepping through a door,
casting off from the shore.
If innocence is found in numbers, what of our hearts?
Asking him after weeks spent measuring
each other's passion
             for distance

Heavenly perspectives

i

God explains:
You think it starts and ends with Me
but you are present too,
in egg and shell; in Antonello's mother
who padlocked her son to her side
with one raised finger
as if she was moulding space
out of the air

You are the blue glint in the rock,
you are the Persian miners, tuned to light
as a dog to smell,
never telling each other
that sometimes they see a glimmer
that is neither sun nor mineral
as if the dark itself was buckling

ii

Gabriel complains:
You told me to expect terror, a coiling back,
not this slow in-gathering, a gesture
that could have halted armies, parted seas

The Mystery of your Shawl

Sex blue. Birth blue.
      Decades of exactitude
to slot you into
      your surrogate cloister,
renunciation in your DNA
      and his. He even chose
a celibate apprentice.
      So why that carnal gush?
The bottega facing north, the door
      ajar, beyond,
the mongrel prairies
      that are neither sea nor river,
parallelogram of light
      falling through
open jugular.
      Heretical, dissident,
solid as coral,
      the apprentice wanting
to drive a nail through it.

The Celibate Apprentice

I don't like girls, that's all. Mamma
says it's just a phase. Meanwhile,
I choose not to dabble in the other

Vittoria's nothing special,
plain as a gull with those nun's eyes,
mouth like a twig in winter

But it was hot that summer,
the air a salty soup
and we three, drowning

The only painter I ever met
who craved the dark, turning me
vampire for that vein of lagoon blue

The girl remained impervious,
to light,
to me

But I could feel lust   shorting
between them
                    like a faulty current

Time To Choose

A mistake to go to Palermo in February. Hard to tell
who was sulkier. S, who could have been ski-ing,
or the city, its southern glow snuffed out by rain.

We were quarrelling long before
we stepped into her blue world.

               If there was a moment
when my life turned towards freedom…
though the change was deep and private
as the bend in an underground river,
                             dormant for years.

That morning, I just stared while S grew impatient,
he was dreaming of *pasta alla norma* like his mamma
never made and sunlight – neither of which we found.

Mary, Mary, Quite Contrary

I don't know what you want from me,
and don't say "nothing" – I've heard that before.

Nothing will come of nothing

His favourite sum,
the Ground Zero of virginity.

It's true, I kept myself tidy.

Perhaps I thought my prince would come.
But waiting games are dangerous,

travelling inwards, I entered His blue prairie,

a door marked Solitude,
a room called Bliss

How Does Your Garden Grow?

Walled.
Locked.
Hortus Conclusus.

~

INTERVIEWING DAYANITA SINGH, NEW DELHI 2012

Greeting me alone, in the doorway of her studio. Behind her on the table, books: Ondaatje, Sebald, Calvino. A photographer who sculpts her pictures out of words. "Don't call me an artist; I'm a bookmaker."

Images pouring through her hands like liquid metal. Dipsticks of light plumbing an oil-black corridor. Girl on a bed, bare legs skewed in adolescent anger, her skin a forcefield of longing.

"Is it a poem? A short story? A novella?"

No, it's a *pietà*.

Somewhere between the morning coffee and the fish she grilled as the sky wrung out its last dro of hot blue, D talked of going solo – her realisation that a room of your own is not enough when you have many selves, each demanding a conversation with the other, each clamouring for silence

But I am looking at the tripwire tension in those teenage hips.

Go Away Closer.

Overheard I

"If I hadn't been a dancer,
I would have been a nun."

Darci Kistler, prima ballerina

telling us that what we saw

                               night after night

was not a woman   offering herself up

but one   turning herself inward

guarding her stage like a *hortus conclusus*

reciting her steps like a catechism

counting each beat of her private audience

confessing herself to God or her daemon?

                               duet for one

Overheard II

"If I hadn't been a politican
                 I would have been
a dancer."

Liz Kendall, Labour MP, (August 2015)

FOR FRANCESCA WOODMAN (AFTER ADRIENNE RICH)

The fact of a doorframe
gave you something to hold on to

as you moved through the world skinless,
wearing your broken rooms like water.

You propped Euclid on your pillow,
turned your lens on his mute glass eyes,

finding infinity in fugitive corners,
pockets of grace in imprecise angles,

prowling those parched thresholds
like a cat seeking sunlight,

less narcissist than pilgrim child,
undressing the elements like dolls.

MOORINGS (AFTER ADRIENNE RICH)

The fact of a doorframe
        means there is something
to hold onto with both hands
        when the moon slips
its moorings, falls
        like a cinder caught
in the wind's crossfire,
        a pocket of time and space
that closes as it opens,
        leaving the sea reeling
at its likeness to the sky,
        bone-white skin
cantilevered over waterlight,
        the chimneys dreaming
of an afterlife as spires

BADLANDS

"It's a size you can walk into." Agnes Martin

When I heard that you saw your paintings as thresholds,
I thought of the archways between Virgin and Angel,
as if love was something to pass through.

How grateful we are for strict lines,
thirsty for a grammar of desire,
fearful of that unholy, illiterate blue.

You said your grids were innocent as trees,
pure as our third eye, a way to see
not what you saw but its internal grace.

To me, your lines are holding cells
for rage, graphs for plotting a woman's silence,
jotting her most secret peregrinations,

ciphers for a landscape so dangerous
it can't be given shape:
original, sinless, nothing to confess.

Mary wanders.
Medea waits.
God bless.

FOR NASREEN

"A spider can only make a web but it makes it to perfection," Nasreen Mohamedi

I never met you but I think you rose with the dawn
and napped before sunset, then gathered yourself
for a night at your drawing board,

swirl of fan
beating out the memory
of birds landing on the Kihim coast,

flute notes tracing
the view through the bars
of a balcony

on a day without sunlight,
when there is nothing
to see, anyway.

I could write of your body's betrayal
but your long eyes slide sideways,
of you as woman, solo,

but you gesture to a faith
in love and work.
Reduce. Reduce. Reduce.

FOR ISABEL

I wake to fear and a froth of birdsong,
the curtains swollen with underwater light,
the canal taut as a layer of cellophane.

A painter sends me lines she has written
in a language that I do not speak
knowing I have the root to hand.

Certain words reveal themselves like flowers,
others clasp their provenance bud-tight.
I map a course across the Mediterranean,

out-running my own demons in pursuit
of another woman's fantasy
as the sky thickens, poised for thunder

Song for a Lost Girl

Watch her as she walks, hips true as bells,
the swing and sway of them sets windows
rattling, shakes the oldest trees, her face carved
with razor blades and all the blood kept somewhere else.
Someone warns her the body has a memory
but she is done remembering.
Every morning she makes her peace with what remains
after the dark has fed, grateful that leftovers
cannot be hungry, cleansing herself in the innocence
of sidewalks, takeaway coffee like a holy offering,
praise song of car horns honouring her,
their commuter priestess!
Watch her — if Rumi's right and wounds are
where the light comes in, she is all shimmer

ON ST PETER HEALING THE SICK WITH HIS SHADOW

He doesn't look, the saint, just walks on by,
his gaze on some distant point within, a place
where love breeds miracles. His feet can
channel God. Two wolf-grey bands closing
the prayer begun by wall and window jamb,
lines clean as shooting stars and leaving less
to chance. The supplicants thirsting for Peter's
negative, his darker self, the little friend called
Absence. We think of light as our Redeemer but
even messiahs check out. The man in the black hat
steps in. Here and there, invalids rise.

Hyde Park Sonnet

Friday evening, West Carriage Drive. The Shard
on the horizon, as if the river were dammed
with smoke. Light like Roman glass dug up after
centuries. Only in September, these fermented sunsets.
There's a conversation I'm not having here and
its whisper is drowning out the hum of evening.
I thought it was with you: the stammer of love,
poetry, illness, exile. But there's more. A heron
perches on a shoreline stake, the weave of her wings
mapping the grain of the wood. It's not about innocence
or guilt; those fantasies of purity are why we're stranded.
It's fearing that you're being deafened. The heron opens
her wings. Hears the ligaments of oak flex to her
recalibrated weight. Such quiet, conciliatory movements.

CHRISTMAS QUARREL

New Year's Day, Battersea Park,
trees gleaming under sleeves of frost.
So once you shone when I drew near,
love coming off you like static.
Now you're holed up in memory's lair,
gnawing at your wounds to keep them raw,
and I'm… above me, a sudden froth of green.
Parrots! Second generation now, but still
that lime-bright shade is marvellous
among our northern blues and greys.
Difficult not to see them as messengers,
come to spread the word that
anything is possible: peace in the Middle East,
a surfeit of pandas, sorry.

FURIES

A week that began
with my anger
at your failure
to provide
insulation

            the tail-end of Gertrude whistling under
            your clapped-out windows

Wednesday, we're at the British Museum
you're turning the lives of the Pharoahs
into stories of your childhood and I'm still
snarling

both of us deaf to a people
who preserved not only the bodies of their dead

but also their shadows

Friday night brings armistice

David Attenborough discovering the world's largest dinosaur

ferrous-red thigh-bone as big as a pony

Faced with a hundred million years ago

and Imogen hurling *craquelures* of rain
against the window

what can we do but reach for each other?

3am, I draw back the curtain, call
light for our shadow

FISHING IN THE DODECANESE

Mid-afternoon, sea like blue oil,
       land cancelled, memory
cancelled. All that remains
       are our hands, your walnut
knuckles, my fingers smaller,
       more supple.
Between us, tangle.
       The line coiled badly
and too long neglected,
       each knot clenched
tight and damp
       with seawater, still,
after months. You're passing me
       one end, and I am wriggling
my nail under one taut,
       unyielding crest of thread.
To feel it loosen
       is to die a little.

LETTER FROM THE PELOPONNESE

A week now that I have been sealed
into the paperweight world of the sailboat.
Waking to light like a bird of prey –
poised, hovering, stealing
its skin from rock and water.

I glimpse you as if through a telescope.
A man for whom freedom is a watchword,
with all the vigilance that implies.
Both rogue and stray, less absent than elsewhere,
always on the edge of leaving.

You would hear holy songs in the goat bells;
sacred rhythms in the whirr of the cicadas.
When you play, your fingers weave prayer carpets
of sound out of shapes no-one else can see.
Your music has hollowed me to the language of the morning.

At home you ask for silence as if it were a hymn
so that our rooms are shrines to cussing engines,
birdsong, our voices plaiting through open doorways.
Invisible braids of daily, stubborn listening
that haunt the house long after we are gone.

BREAKFAST WITH PALESTRINA

Clouds on fast-forward
    after a night of gales,
headache-blue sky,
    one of us needing sex,
the other stillness.
    Thank god for a composer
who quarried vowels
    from Lazio's sandstone light,
membrane of sound,
    contracting, expanding,
uncanny wings spreading
    under the burden of weightlessness.
You feel the effort.
    Flight *en pointe*.
The rolled-gold leap
    of resurrection, beaten, wound

NOTES

BIRD OF SORROW I
The title comes from a song by Irish singer/songwriter Glen Hansard.

BIRD OF SORROW II (MEDEA'S SONG)
The phrase 'some idea of happiness' comes from St Augustine's Confessions; 'the blue peninsula' comes from Emily Dickinson's poem no. 404.

GIRL, RISING
This poem was inspired by photographs taken by Dayanita Singh. One shows a young girl apparently levitating on a balcony in Varanasi. The other shows a room in an anonymous state office lined with archives of files.

FUGITIVE
The mosaic of the Madonna and Child in the cathedral of Torcello, in the Venice lagoon, is based on an earlier model, known as a Hodgeteria — She who shows the way — that, legend has it, was painted by St Luke.

AFTER YOU'D GONE
The phrase 'the blue way out of here' comes from Michael Ondaatje's poem 'Rock Bottom'; the line 'fluid … blood' comes from "The Archetypes and the Collective Unconscious by C.G Jung

PALERMO SUITE
This sequence was inspired by a painting entitled the Virgin of the Annunciation by the Sicilian artist Antonello da Messina (c1430 -1479). It hangs in Palazzo Abatellis, the Regional Gallery of Art in Palermo, Sicily.

INTERVIEWING DAYANITA SINGH, NEW DELHI 2012
Dayanita Singh, b.1961 New Delhi, is an artist. Her medium is photography and the book is her primary form. Go Away Closer is the title of one of her books.

BADLANDS
Agnes Martin (1912-2004) was an American abstract artist who worked primarily with the grid.

FOR NASREEN
Born in Karachi, then India now Pakistan, in 1937, Nasreen Mohamedi was an abstract artist who worked in pencil and pen and ink. She died in 1990.

FOR FRANCESCA WOODMAN
Francesca Woodman was an American photographer (1958-1981) primarily known for black and white photographs of herself in interior settings. She lived in Italy for the last years of her life before tragically killing herself at the age of 22.

FOR ISABEL
Isabel Ramoneda Violan is a Spanish abstract artist based in Barcelona

ON ST PETER HEALING THE SICK
This poem was inspired by a fresco entitled "St Peter Healing the Sick with his Shadow" by the 15th-century Florentine painter Masaccio. It is part of a cycle he painted for the Brancacci Chapel in the Church of Santa Maria del Carmine in Florence.